"The world breaks everyone, and afterward, many are strong at the broken places."

— Ernest Hemingway

THE *DRIFT* EFFECT

THE SCIENCE BEHIND LIFE'S CHAOS AND BEHAVIORS THAT BRING ORDER

PATRICK BURNS

Copyright © 2025 Patrick Burns
All rights reserved. No part of this book may be reproduced, stored in a retrieval system, or transmitted in any form or by any means including electronic, mechanical, photocopying, recording, or otherwise, without prior written permission from the author, except in the case of brief quotations used in reviews or scholarly works.

ISBN: 979-8-9943024-9-1
Cover Design: Generated by OpenAI
Illustrations: Generated by OpenAI
Published by: Independently Published

This book is a work of nonfiction. While the research, studies, and scientific principles referenced are real, the anecdotes and metaphors reflect the author's personal perspective. This book is not intended to provide medical, psychological, legal, or financial advice. Always consult a qualified professional when making decisions affecting your health, safety, or finances.

Printed in The United States of America

Dedicated to my family

The people who make the drift worth fighting

CONTENTS

Introduction

Chapter 01: What is Entropy?

Chapter 02: How is Drift Different?

Chapter 03: The Single Dirty Dish

Chapter 04: Mental Drift

Chapter 05: Health Drift

Chapter 06: Relationship Drift

Chapter 07: Financial Drift

Chapter 08: What Is Negentropy?

Chapter 09: The Role of Information

Chapter 10: Creating Negentropic Behaviors

Chapter 11: The Waiting Game of Success

Chapter 12: The Effect of Identity

Chapter 13: Maintaining a Negentropic Life

Introduction

Drift is a simple term to explain a law of physics that governs every aspect of the world around you, as well as most aspects of your life. When chaos creeps into your life, it's really *ENTROPY* that's causing things to drift from order to disorder. The second law of thermodynamics states that in any closed system, entropy (disorder) will increase or stay neutral, but it will never decrease without external forces.

Imagine spending all day building a sandcastle on the beach. It's perfect. Every grain of sand has been organized to create order and structure. But over time, that perfectly organized structure will slowly start to crumble. The walls weaken. The ocean breeze gradually strips those grains of sand away and gravity pulls them to the earth, until finally, it returns to a disorganized pile of sand again. That is entropy.

But on the flip side, that same disorganized pile of sand will never organize itself into a perfectly formed sandcastle. There are so many aspects of your life that behave the same way. Over time, they erode, until all we are left with is disorder. This book is about recognizing the cracks in your life and creating the negentropic behaviors that will prevent the cracks from forming in the first place to give your "sandcastle of life" stability.

Chapter 01: What is Entropy?

Entropy isn't a philosophical concept; it's part of a scientific *law*. But only a few centuries ago, we didn't have a full understanding of entropy. In fact, we didn't even have a name for it, but we could see its effects. A French engineer named Sadi Carnot was the first one to uncover the problem that led to the discovery of entropy. The problem was that no matter how perfectly designed a steam engine was, it could never be 100% efficient. There was always some loss of energy as heat escaping. In physics, that escaped heat is considered "disorder" because it's dispersed so randomly that it could no longer be used for work. Energy was drifting away, and the engine was leaking "order." This natural drift toward disorder was the first clue to the force of entropy, but it wasn't until years later that a German physicist Rudolf Clausius would name that force entropy (from "*energy*" and the Greek "*trope*" meaning "transformation") and determine the calculations to quantify it. Engineers and scientists can now use those formulas to calculate everything from nuclear waste container degradation to prescription expiration.

Without precise calculations of entropy, scientists wouldn't be able to predict the failure of nuclear waste barrels. They calculate it to estimate how fast heat spreads through the barrel and when the metal will weaken and crack from thermal stress. Pharmaceutical companies model entropy in drug molecules of their medication. This helps them determine what type of packaging the medication needs, as well as what temperature it should be stored at and when it will expire. And did you know that museums storing classic cars have to change the tires every few years even though they never get used? If they don't, the tires can blow out. You can blame entropy for that one too. Chemists can track how oxygen breaks down polymer chains in car tires. That breakdown will cause stored tires to weaken, but not show any of the normal signs of wear, like cracking and fading. Entropy is working in silence, waiting to cause chaos.

That might make entropy seem pretty ominous, but it's also pretty incredible. It's the very reason we understand the direction of time. Think about this: if I played you a video of hundreds of shards of glass spread across a table that suddenly come together to form a beautiful vase, you would immediately know which direction that video was playing… reversed. How did you know that? It just seems obvious, but the reason is entropy. Because without energy, in any closed system, entropy only *grows*. Order naturally moves toward chaos, and entropy determines the direction of time. We see time as a flowing river moving in one direction, but for almost all laws of physics, at a fundamental level, time doesn't really matter. At least not which direction it flows. You can run the math with time running in either direction and you get the same answer. That's why one of the only reasons physicists can prove that time flows in a single direction is because they can observe *entropy*. So if we can just remove entropy… boom… time travel. No flux capacitor needed. Joking aside, quantum physicists have been able to send heat flowing "backwards in time" by manipulating entropy. Instead of heat moving from hot to cold, like it naturally does over time, they produced a microscopic two-particle system where normal flow could be reversed. They did that by injecting quantum correlations into the system, which caused entropy to be reduced artificially[1]. For us non-quantum physicists, it flipped time's direction at a quantum level and heat flowed from cold to hot. "Microscopic heat time travel."

---

[1] Micadei, K., et al. "Reversing the Thermodynamic Arrow of Time Using Quantum Correlations." Communications Physics, vol. 2, 2019, pp. 1–6, doi:10.1038/s42005-019-0245-0

Time isn't the only direction that entropy controls. It also controls the direction of your life. It guides you to who you become in the future, but in this case, the direction it's constantly pulling you is down. That's why we need to act against it, because just like those stored tires, systems that look fine from the outside can be deteriorating inside without you knowing. And by the time you realize something's wrong, it's too late. In your life, entropy acts in the exact same way, just called a different name… *DRIFT*.

Chapter 02: How is Drift Different?

Drift is the same concept as entropy, but instead of how entropy affects our natural world with things like metal degradation, now we're talking about how drift affects our social world with life's degradation. Drift is what happens to our own personal sandcastle when it's left in the elements and eroding from the forces of nature. Drift is also an equal opportunity destroyer. It doesn't discriminate or play favorites. It will take down anyone, anywhere, without prejudice. It also infects every aspect of our life. Our mind, our body, our relationships, and even our finances. And left unchecked, it will spread across these areas like wildfire.

And just like wildfire, drift is a force of nature. Wildfires destroy. It's in their nature. If a homeowner loses their house in a wildfire, they don't blame themselves for allowing the flames to destroy it. There's no guilt felt. So why would you let yourself feel guilty about allowing drift to destroy your life? It's just another part of nature, and you are always going to be in a constant battle with the forces of nature. Don't feel guilt or self-pity. It's not that you lack discipline or are lazy, and it's not a character flaw. It's just nature returning the world to its natural state of disorder.

Since the natural state of the world is disorder, it makes sense that it's easier for our life to naturally slide toward chaos. There are just more chaotic opportunities. Think about it, right now, in this very moment, how many things could you do that would make your life worse? By the end of the day you could be in jail, or the hospital, or talking to a divorce lawyer, or dead. Even something less serious like a bad post on social media could get you in trouble. There was a time in society when celebrities were scrutinizing every post they made because cancel culture was destroying careers left and right, over posts that were made years prior. There are almost endless possibilities of things that could make your life significantly worse by the end of the day. But how many things could you do, at this very second, to make your life significantly better by the end of the day? Not many.

Physicists can prove that the natural drift toward chaos isn't psychological, it's mathematical. It was Austrian physicist Ludwig Boltzmann who discovered why entropy behaves this way, and he did it by posing a very simple question... Why does chaos always win? The answer is simple and it's directly tied to what we just discussed. Chaos is statistically more likely. There are way more ways for a system to be disorganized than organized. Boltzmann realized that order is rare in the natural world and chaos is common. He created an equation that quantified that quality: $S = k \log W$. He put that equation on his tombstone, which I think is fitting because it shows that in the end, our bodies will return to the earth and entropy will win. Like it always does.

The fact that our lives naturally drift toward chaos is probably why most of the energy that we exert is spent avoiding pain, not seeking gains. That fact is shown most clearly in a study from 1979. In this study, psychologists Daniel Kahneman and Amos Tversky learned that subjects were twice as emotionally motivated to avoid losses than to pursue gains[2]. They gave subjects opportunities to either gain or lose $100. But even when the odds were stacked in favor of winning, the subjects would still choose the option that minimized their risk of loss. Risk aversion is biologically ingrained into our DNA, and it's kept us safe and alive for thousands of years, but it can also work against us when it comes time to capitalize on riskier opportunities. The trick is to leverage the

---

[2] Kahneman, D., & Tversky, A. (1979). Prospect theory: An analysis of decision under risk. Econometrica, 47(2), 263–291.

systems that you've built. That minimizes your risk, so capitalizing on those opportunities feels more comfortable. You don't want the improvement of your life to take a backseat, because you're too distracted by trying to keep it together.

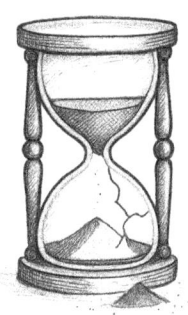

Chapter 03: The Single Dirty Dish

I remember the first time I lived alone in college and had the freedom to be as clean or messy as I wanted. No parents, roommates, or girlfriends telling me how to live. This is when I really saw drift with my own eyes. My apartment would have a continual ebb and flow of filth. First there would be a catalyst event that would put me into cleaning mode. A guest would be coming to visit, so I would spend the entire afternoon scrubbing the place top to bottom, making it spotless. It felt great afterwards, and for the next few days I would continue to keep it spotless. I'd clean the toilet bowl after every use, wash every dish immediately, and make my bed every morning. But after a few days, I'd start to let things slide. A single dirty dish would be left in the sink. My drift always started with that *single dirty dish* in the sink. That was the spark that lit the fuse. My catalyst. After the dish I'd leave my bed unmade… "because if I'm going to mess it up in a couple hours when I go back to sleep, what's the point of making it right now?" And by that time, I'd completely given up on any sort of bathroom hygiene. So the filth slowly crept in, but once it did become noticeable, it was way easier to add a little more to it without feeling guilty… "because what's one more dish when there's already a huge pile?"

Over the next four chapters, we will look at how drift can creep into your mind, body, relationships, and finances. How it goes unnoticed at first, and the ripple effects it has on other areas. I will reference this single dirty dish metaphor for actions that are catalysts for drift starting to take hold. These are actions that usually get brushed off as insignificant. Your first job will be to find your own personal "single dirty dish" in each area so you can identify *your* drift early. Later you will develop the tools needed to create behaviors that will stop the drift from starting in the first place.

Chapter 04: Mental Drift

Drift in the form of clutter doesn't just infect your home. It will spread to your mind too. The old saying of "a cluttered desk, a cluttered mind" rings very true to me. I focus better and feel more motivated and productive when the space around me is clean and tidy. But our minds themselves can collect clutter over time. In today's digital age, our minds are being bombarded with content that's fighting for our attention. And as we constantly shift our attention from one piece of content to another, over and over again, our minds begin to train themselves to limit focus to shorter periods of time. This ongoing attention shift causes something psychologists call "attention residue." Studies show that constant small distractions create a measurable drag on your focus and clarity[3]. It was harder for participants to complete a new task if they were interrupted while working on a previous one. Part of their attention was still lingering on the first task, and it was difficult for them to fully engage in the new one. Researchers realized that the effect was even worse if the participant felt that the original task had been left unfinished or unresolved. It stuck in their minds more. But strangely, they didn't notice a thing. The researchers could see a measurable drop in their scores, but the participants claimed they felt no difference in their cognitive abilities. The mental drift went completely unnoticed to those participants, but it still left clutter in their mind, just like that dirty dish in the sink.

Even decisions themselves can act as mental clutter that paralyzes our future choices. It's yet another form of drift causing silent chaos in the background. Have you had a busy day with tons of interactions, micro-

---

[3] Leroy, S. (2009). Why is it so hard to do my work? The challenge of attention residue when switching between work tasks. Organizational Behavior and Human Decision Processes, 109(2), 168–181. https://doi.org/10.1016/j.obhdp.2009.04.002

decisions, mental hurdles, and by the time you get home, your brain is too fried to even decide what to eat for dinner? This is another effect of mental drift, and it happens to us all the time. In fact, this effect has even determined people's very freedom. Researchers at Columbia University found that judges were more likely to deny parole to prisoners seen later in the day.[4] Early in the morning an inmate would have a 65% chance to be paroled, but later in the day, it dropped to near zero. Unless it followed a break or meal, then the chances went back up. The judges weren't seeing more qualified parolees in the morning. There was another factor at play. The decisions made in the morning acted like mental clutter, filling up the mind. By midday so much had accumulated that the brain defaulted to the safest, easiest path… just say no. Easy, no need to think. Then after a break or meal, rest would recover some of that mental capacity. They were now able to make rational decisions again, instead of reverting back to the default *no*. If you learn nothing else from this book, at least you now know the best time of day to apply for parole. Totally worth the read.

One way people fight mental drift is by reducing attention residue with meditation, and there are a lot of different forms. For some people, yoga is their form of meditation, but for others it's gardening. Even spending 10 minutes alone before work to gather your thoughts can help. If it relaxes you and brings your mind peace, it's working. Meditation through breathing exercises has helped me a lot in the past. For a while I followed the practices of Wim Hof, because of his expertise in breathing. He's a fascinating man that has done some amazing things in his life. One of Wim's

---

[4] Danziger, S., Levav, J., & Avnaim-Pesso, L. (2011). Extraneous factors in judicial decisions. Proceedings of the National Academy of Sciences, 108(17), 6889–6892. https://doi.org/10.1073/pnas.1018033108

more extreme claims was that he was able to control his autonomic nervous system using his deep power-breath technique. The "auto" or "automatic" part of the name will tell you that this is a part of the body we typically don't control, so scientists were ready to debunk his outrageous claim. In 2014 researchers at Radboud University ran tests on Wim that may seem a little extreme[5]. They injected him with E. coli endotoxin. That's really bad for the body. It causes severe symptoms like fever, chills, nausea, inflammation… but not with Wim. Scientists were shocked to see that after using his breathing techniques, his physiological response caused his adrenaline to spike, lowering inflammation and reducing his symptoms. But those scientists just chalked it up to good genes. They assumed genetics must be the explanation, until Wim brought in 12 random strangers, spent four days training them to breathe, and repeated the experiment with similar results. No tricks. No genetic advantage. Just breathing. Since breathing is something you do every day, and you're really good at it, it's an easy form of meditation to reverse mental drift's effects. Just a few minutes of controlled breathing can remove that mental residue and lower your stress, giving you the reset you need to keep drift at bay.

All of these examples of mental drift can spread to other parts of your life, too. Stress from mental drift can lead to physical symptoms like migraines or insomnia. Physical health can be affected by drift in other ways too. In the next chapter we'll explore some of those ways.

---

[5] Kox, M. et al. "Voluntary Activation of the Sympathetic Nervous System and Attenuation of the Innate Immune Response in Humans." Proceedings of the National Academy of Sciences, 2014.

Chapter 05: Health Drift

The most obvious example to see drift's effect on health is with exercise. A lot of new gym routines start strong in the beginning, but fade out quickly. Go take a look at how busy your local gym is right after New Year's, and then check back in April. Those health-based New Year's resolutions rarely last past the first quarter of the year. But most of the people that stopped going to the gym didn't go from five days a week to zero overnight. They started going five days a week, then skipped just one day during their second week, and since their birthday was the following week, they missed two days for that. By week four it went down to twice a week, and a month later it's only once every other week. Finally, they just stop going completely. Drift won that battle.

Researchers found that the degree to which this is happening is probably higher than you might think[6]. In 2021 they analyzed members of two different gyms and found that after a year, less than 20% of the members were still continuing to go. The other 80%+ had slowly dropped out. The dropout rate followed the same pattern that we have been discussing with drift itself. Not all at once, but slowly and silently over time. This study also illustrates the fact that drift isn't a personal failure, but something that is statistically impossible to avoid unless you create behaviors that counter it.

Diet is another obvious example of how drift can deteriorate health. My wife is Mexican, and she shared with me a saying in Spanish that I love. "Uno no es

---

[6] Storer, T. W., Dallinga, J. M., & Lemmink, K. A. P. M. (2021). Dropout predictors at gyms: A retrospective study. International Journal of Environmental Research and Public Health, 18(17), 9054. https://doi.org/10.3390/ijerph18179054

ninguno." It's fun to say, it rhymes, but the meaning is even better. It roughly translates to "one isn't anything." Most of the time I heard it said to me in Mexico was when I was being offered an alcoholic beverage. But I went and applied this philosophy to food… for years! It's just one piece of cake for dessert. Or just one cookie. Or just one *pack* of cookies. Uno no es ninguno. But that is a slippery slope and drift compounds. So over the first couple of years of being married my body fat percentage doubled. But it also wasn't quick. First my pants started to feel a little snug, and then a little tight, then really tight, and then buttons started to pop. Drift is sneaky. The worst part is, the people around you usually don't start making comments until it's an obvious problem. By the time my wife started telling me to eat more veggies and put the cookies down, I was already *way* overweight. And I struggled with my weight for a long time, because I would try exciting new diets and routines that would get me to my goal quickly, but it wouldn't be something that I could maintain for the long term. So I'd shed the pounds in a flash, but gain them all right back when I stopped maintaining the diet. And the truth is, the super quick, up and down, yo-yo-type weight loss is really unhealthy. Our bodies actually interpret it as a form of stress. But luckily, after years of experimenting, I finally found a behavior that was easy and manageable. It's something that I've maintained for years now and most importantly, I feel it'll be easy to maintain that behavior in the future.

Another danger with diet is that even if you don't feel like you're overeating by very much, it can become a serious problem that will show up on the scale in the future. Researchers found that just a small consistent calorie increase contributes to slow but steady weight gain[7]. Metabolic modelers can calculate the amount of daily calories needed to drastically change weight over time, and it's not much. Only an extra 100 calories. That's it. An extra cookie after dinner would do the trick. Although that doesn't seem like much, it can account for an extra 10 pounds of fat every year. The problem is, when you get a surplus of calories from eating an extra cookie every night, your body doesn't suddenly decide to burn an extra cookie's worth of calories just because you had the munchies. It stores that surplus to use later, and usually, it stores it as fat. So that one extra cookie really does make a difference when it becomes something you permit regularly day after day.

Health is controlled by drift in many different ways. And although diet and exercise can sometimes feel like work, the body requires that work to thrive. If it doesn't get consistent work, it can become obese, malnourished, or muscles start to deteriorate when atrophy sets in. The relationships in our life also need constant work so they don't suffer from atrophy, just like our bodies. In the next chapter we will explore how drift causes our relationships to… drift.

---

[7] Hall, K. D., & Kahan, S. (2018). Maintenance of lost weight and long-term management of obesity. Gastroenterology, 152(7), 1729–1738.

Chapter 06: Relationship Drift

Drift causes relationships to deteriorate over time if they're not fed the attention they deserve. Most adults have close friends from their past whom they've lost touch with and it's almost never on bad terms or from one specific moment. Time just went by and phone calls got fewer and fewer. That's the single dish in the sink. Drift crept in. Then they got married and had a kid or two and you don't even know their spouse's or kid's name. So you feel even more distant. Now it's too late. Drift did what it does best and eroded the relationship, just like the walls of your sandcastle.

There are also micro-behaviors that can erode relationships at their core, slowly over time. These are not major betrayals or abuses. They are subtle. Almost dismissible. Nevertheless, they kill relationships right under our noses. Relationship researchers John and Julie Gottman were able to narrow down these actions to four main behaviors. By observing these four behaviors, they were able to predict divorce rates with 90% accuracy. They called them "The Four Horsemen of the Apocalypse": criticism, defensiveness, stonewalling, and contempt.[8] These behaviors, especially contempt, slowly eat away at relationships and bring them crumbling down. Not quickly, but over months or years of constant accumulation.

To see what relationship drift looks like, we can look at the marriage of two celebrities, Gwyneth Paltrow and Chris Martin from Coldplay. Their failed marriage wasn't the cause of a singular dramatic event. No betrayal or blowout. Gwyneth said in multiple interviews that their relationship had slowly diminished over time. She mentioned there were years when they weren't communicating well. Small misunderstandings

---

[8] Gottman, J. M. (1994). What predicts divorce? The relationship between marital processes and marital outcomes. Psychology Press.

piled up and phone calls were left unreturned. Gradually their relationship slipped into a friendship instead of a marriage. She said that when the split eventually happened, it felt like an acceptance of a truth that had been building silently over time.

Some relationship drift can feel harmless or it won't feel like anything at all. It's nothing big, like an unreturned missed call, or a sarcastic or dismissive comment, or maybe you flake on plans because something else came up. And maybe you're right to think it's not a big deal. But it does compound, just like clutter. And just like the pasta sauce on that dirty dish, the longer it's left there, the harder it is to clean up. Sometimes though, relationships *do* end in a ball of flame. A huge catastrophic event that would easily explain the demise of the relationship. But if we did a full autopsy on that breakup, we'll usually find that there were years of drift eroding the foundation, and that blow-up event was an inevitable ending.

Look back on your life and think about the friends that you once had. Did the friendship end abruptly, or did it die slowly? Do you feel that one of you is to blame or did it feel unintentional? As you drifted further apart, did it become harder to come back together? In hindsight, was there something you could have done to prevent that relationship from deteriorating? Now that you understand how drift works and how it causes relationships to crumble, you can recognize the cracks and build the support to keep them together.

Chapter 07: Financial Drift

When I was younger I would play the "don't look" game with my finances. I would start out the month with a good paycheck and know exactly how much money I had in the bank. Then I would overspend on a shopping spree or lose more than I planned at the casino. At that point, I wouldn't know exactly how much I had in the bank and I'd start playing Russian roulette with my debit card at the checkout counter. On more than one occasion, I've had the embarrassing experience of holding up a store line to return cans of beans and ramen noodles that I couldn't pay for. The truth is, I could have checked my balance at any time and gotten my finances in order. But once things started to spiral, I got overwhelmed and just wanted to stick my head in the sand. Later I found out that behavioral economists call this "the ostrich effect," for that exact reason[9]. People check their finances way less often when they think it's going to be bad news. As a more mature adult, I've come to learn how to spot "the dish in the sink." For me, with finances, it's overspending on something big. That's my single dirty dish starting the spiral.

There's another psychological effect that's controlling our financial futures without us knowing. Consumer psychologists call this the "small leak effect" or "the latte effect."[10] It happens when we have lots of small, but consistent, purchases that go untracked because of their insignificance. Maybe it's the daily latte you order, or the fifteen different video streaming services

---

[9] Karlsson, N., Loewenstein, G., & Seppi, D. (2009). The ostrich effect: Selective attention to information. Journal of Risk and Uncertainty, 38(2), 95–115. https://doi.org/10.1007/s11166-009-9060-6

[10] Soman, D., & Cheema, A. (2011). Earmarking and financial behavior. Journal of Marketing Research, 48(SPL), S78–S94.

you signed up for. Drift loves infiltrating when we aren't tracking or paying attention to it. Individually, these purchases are minor, but when you add them up, they become significant enough to delay people's long-term financial goals. Researchers found that if money hasn't been earmarked for a specific purpose, it tends to go toward whatever gives us immediate gratification. And a lot of things that give us immediate gratification, aren't good for our long-term benefit.

Another study illustrating that effect showed that two-thirds of participants couldn't list every single active subscription they had, and most of them significantly underestimated their total monthly spending[11]. There were even subscriptions they were paying for, but had no memory of signing up for. This piece of information isn't lost on these big companies, and it's one of the reasons that the subscription model has become so popular with big business. The tiny silent automatic payments go unnoticed and the companies drain you slowly every month.

Small purchases compounding into something major hit that same theme that has been threaded throughout this book. Drift is small and compounding. But it all starts with a single purchase of a latte, or a single unpaid overdue bill, or whatever your single dirty dish is. Don't let them pile up.

---

[11] Clemes, M. D., Gan, C., & Zhang, J. (2014). Consumer subscription services and expenditure underestimation. Journal of Consumer Affairs, 48(1), 83–109.

Chapter 08: What Is Negentropy?

Understanding how to identify the single dirty dish is an important first step, but what you do next is what really matters. The only thing to fight drift, or entropy, is with *NEGENTROPY*. Learning to create negentropic behaviors is the key to maintaining order.

If you haven't guessed already, negentropy is the opposite of entropy. In nature, energy is needed when things go from a disorganized state to an organized state. Life is no different. Without energy, structure can't be sustained.

The concept of negentropy was first described in *What is Life?* by physicist Erwin Schrödinger. That's the same famous, 'dead cat in a box' physicist you learned about in school. He described how living systems used energy to avoid decay and thus negate entropy… *negative entropy*. Organisms consume high-quality energy with low entropy like sunlight and food, and convert that into organized structure like DNA and cells.

A plant takes the raw chaotic energy of the sun and uses it to create structure and form within its cellular walls. It grows toward that light with purpose and has a pure, organized form. But if you remove the sun and rob it of its source of energy, that plant will slowly wither and die, returning to the earth just like the sandcastle. The same is true in our bodies. Our damaged cells are constantly being repaired and replaced by our bodies using the energy that we consume. If we stop consuming the food that provides the energy to repair cells, the system starts to fail and we take the path of the plant and the sandcastle.

The systems you will create to combat entropy will be similar to the systems that exist in the natural world. Nature's systems don't rely on habits, and neither should you. A migrating flock of birds doesn't rely on habits or motivation from their fellow birds. They are driven by instinctive behavior guided by natural cues like solar positioning, magnetic fields and temperature. And even when something like a storm pushes the flock off track, they can micro-adjust to stop drift and bring them back on course. That isn't from habits, it's behavior. Behavior comes naturally. You don't need to put conscious effort into behavior because it just flows without thinking. That's the system that you need to emulate. One that has removed all difficult effort until you are left with simple basic natural behaviors that help you defeat the constant pull of drift.

When I mentioned Schrödinger's concept of negative entropy earlier, I left out the last part of the concept. Organisms use energy to maintain order within themselves, but that entropy isn't destroyed in the process. It's pushed outward into the environment. The "cost" is exported. This comes in the form of the CO_2 that we exhale into the air, or the heat our bodies give off, or the waste our organs expel. All of these things are disorder being dumped into the world, so our internal systems can stay ordered. And this is the most important part. Life doesn't destroy entropy, it just moves it somewhere else.

The systems you are creating aren't eliminating that entropy either. It's just being shifted to parts of your life where it creates less friction. When I lay out my clothes the night before, that was the entropy I had to shift. It was the exported "cost." I still had to pay, but instead of "frantic, morning me" doing the task, I exported that cost to "calm, night-before me". A lot of the behaviors I find myself doing were created for present-me to keep *future-me* happy. Suffering a little now so future-me can have it a little easier. My daughter, on the other hand, tends to treat her future-self like garbage. She's constantly choosing the instant gratification that she knows is going to come back to bite her down the road. I joke that if she ever met her future-self in real life, that girl would probably want to kick her present-self's ass. How do you treat your *future-self?* Are you choosing the instant gratification and kicking the can down the road? Instant gratification can sometimes be entropy in disguise, causing chaos in the future.

If you were hoping this book would help you find a way to organize your life without any effort, unfortunately the laws of physics won't allow it. This book is here to help you use that energy efficiently so you can disperse entropy to moments that cause less friction. That way, you don't feel it as much.

Chapter 09: The Role of Information

Although Schrödinger came up with the concept of negative entropy, it was actually another scientist who coined the term "negentropy" a few years later. Leon Brillouin was a French-American physicist that worked on quantum mechanics, solid-state physics, information theory, and thermodynamics. It was his merging of thermodynamics and information theory that led him to the mathematical conclusion that when information increases, uncertainty decreases, and reducing uncertainty leads to reduced entropy. To simplify… gaining information reduces entropy.

Without going down a quantum physics rabbit hole of probability and computational thermodynamics, let's just look at the metaphor we've been using. Information reduces drift. Before someone has identified their "single dirty dish," their life just seems chaotic. They might blame bad luck, or lack of discipline, or lack of direction. Maybe they are cleaning, but in all the wrong places. They're trying to fix the wrong problems and spending a lot of energy with very few results. But once they've identified their single dirty dish, the one catalytic moment that starts the drift, they've gained *information*. That information instantly reduces disorder in the system by giving proper direction to their energy. Negentropy increases and drift subsides. Information doesn't eliminate effort, but it does make energy more efficient by helping remove some of the opportunity for wrong decisions.

Waze is a perfect example of a company creating negentropy from information. Driving in Los Angeles in the 90s was a lot more chaotic than today. People would have no idea how long it would take them to make it to work, so they would either leave ridiculously early, just in case, or risk the high stress of trying to fight through rush hour traffic, scrambling to make it on time. Waze took away all that chaos with a few simple pieces of information: real-time traffic, optimal driving routes, and accurate arrival times. Now we know exactly how long it will take us to get to work and the fastest way to get there. The information we've gained from Waze has created negentropy in our daily commute.

Prior to the B-17 bomber, Boeing had released a prototype, the Model 299. This aircraft was the most advanced piece of machinery the world had ever seen. It was able to do things that no other aircraft was capable of. It was larger and faster than its competitors, which is hard to accomplish at the same time. Unfortunately though, all of these technological advances came with increased complexity. Pilots were now required to memorize new procedures, buttons and levers they'd never seen before. Even the country's best pilots struggled with this new technology. In fact, during a demonstration flight in October of 1935, one of the world's top aviators at the time, Major Ployer Hill, lost control of the Model 299 and tragically lost his life in the crash. Investigators later found out that it wasn't equipment malfunction or a lack of the pilot's skill. He just forgot to release a control mechanism. The system was too complicated, and it was too much to remember. The Army Air Corps regrettably told Boeing that as amazing as their plane was, it was too much plane for one man. But instead of scrapping the plans, Boeing came up with a simple but elegant solution. Give the pilots more information. Give them a checklist. They created a one-page checklist that changed everything. The plane flew 1.8 million miles without a serious accident and led to the creation of one of the most successful aircraft in history, the B-17. But without a simple checklist, it might never have existed.

The final piece of the information puzzle is accuracy. The information has to be accurate or it can actually be worse than no information at all. The problem with having wrong information is that you focus your energy on the wrong path. One of the most *expensive* examples of bad information leading to catastrophic consequences cost about $327 million dollars. Ouch. In 1999 the United States had NASA send a spacecraft to orbit Mars and study its weather. Two teams were calculating the trajectory of the Mars Climate Orbiter, but they were using two different units of measurement: metric (newtons) and imperial (pound-force). That wrong information caused the spacecraft to overshoot its target by 170 km and disintegrate into the Martian atmosphere. It wasn't because of a lack of information, it was from bad information.

Chapter 10: Creating Negentropic Behaviors

Now that you understand the relationship between negentropy and energy, how can you use this knowledge to help avoid the chaos that invades your life? The first thing to understand is that in nature, negentropy is rarely loud and obvious. Micro-corrections and smaller systems are usually what win. Look at a beehive. Scientists found that one reason that a beehive stays at a stable temperature is because the individual bees are making micro-adjustments to their organic air-conditioning system[12]. The bees can adjust the temperature of the hive by flapping their wings to cool it, or adjusting their positions for better air circulation, or clustering their bodies together to drive up heat. The adjustments are never major, but they keep the hive from drifting into dangerous conditions.

In your life, you also need to create micro-behaviors that keep you from drifting into dangerous conditions. The first rule you should take from nature is to *keep things small*. Micro-adjustments. When you start to think about what behaviors you want to introduce, remember to make them so small that they're almost unnoticeable. Rinsing off a single dish after I eat isn't overwhelming. It's just one small thing. But staring at a week's worth of dishes piled up in the sink… that makes my blood pressure spike.

These behaviors you're creating also need to be easy. When you adjust a behavior to make things easier, that trains your brain to make that new action its default behavior. Your brain only accounts for 2% of your body weight, but consumes an average of 20% of your

---

[12] Fahrenholz, L., Lamprecht, I., & Schricker, B. (1989). Thermoregulation in the honeybee colony (Apis mellifera). Journal of Comparative Physiology B, 159(5), 551–560.

body's energy.[13] That's why it's always looking for ways to conserve energy, and given any two paths, it will always choose the path of least resistance. The easier path. So when you create your behavior, it should always be the easier of the two paths. If it isn't easy, your brain will just revert to the original path and the behavior won't change.

Just because the action is small, doesn't mean the results can't be significant. You wouldn't think that taking the stairs at work every day would save you from a heart attack, but it could. In fact, you could be 10% less likely to die from cardiovascular disease if you do. Scientists determined this by doing a massive study in the U.K. measuring tens of thousands of citizens' movement. Participants were given wrist accelerometers that could determine how much they moved, the intensity, frequency, and duration. Scientists focused on small quick bursts of movement, not traditional exercise. Things like taking in the groceries from the car, or walking the kids to school in the morning, or taking the stairs at work. Anything with moderate intensity counted, even if it lasted less than 10 minutes. Small, unnoticeable behaviors that didn't feel like extra work although they were moderately intense. After six to seven years of following these participants, they found the people that did those extra little movements were 6-10% less likely to die from things like stroke and metabolic disease. They were 10%-14% less likely to die from cardiovascular disease... even if they didn't participate in traditional exercise. That research proves, even small changes can work to produce meaningful results.

---

[13] Raichle, M.E., & Gusnard, D.A. Appraising the brain's energy budget. Proceedings of the National Academy of Sciences. 2002; 99(16):10237–10239. doi:10.1073/pnas.172399499

Let's say my issue is that I'm always late to work. Then I need to find ways to make it easier for me to be on time than to be late. When I wake up late, the first feeling I have is anxiety. I then try to jump in the shower and race to get clean, frantically fumble through the drawers to find my toothbrush and toothpaste, and spend time I don't have sifting through wrinkled clothes to finally find a shirt that will work. The next 25 minutes of my commute will be absolute hell because I'm driving like a jerk trying to get to work on time. That used to be me. And it definitely wasn't easy. So I made small changes to my behavior. Now I spend time I DO have the night before sifting through those wrinkled clothes to find a shirt I like. And if there's a wrinkled one that I like better, I have plenty of time to take out the ironing board. I also bought a drawer organizer for the bathroom and organized everything to give it an exact place. Now, I just pull out a single tray and it's all there, neat and tidy, no more frantically fumbling. And since I started to set my alarm 15 minutes earlier, the commute has become really enjoyable. I listen to podcasts and sometimes even take the long way to work just so I can finish. No stress. No hassle. Easy. And that's the key. *Keep things easy*.

Just like entropy compounds over time in silence, little by little, until it's overwhelming… negentropy is the same… but reversed. Those small, insignificant, easy behaviors don't make any difference, unless they're continued and compounded. That's when they start to become visible and create meaningful change. If the bees flap their wings once and then stop, it won't change a thing. But constant flapping and micro-adjustments keep the hive stable. *Keep things consistent because that* consistency creates the stability that prevents drift.

Negentropy isn't about making huge changes. It's actually the opposite. It's making micro-adjustments to maintain systems over long periods of time. It's about creating behaviors that make the right decision the easiest path, creating the least resistance toward order. Small, easy, and consistent.

Chapter 11: The Waiting Game of Success

I mentioned earlier that you shouldn't rely on habits, but why? Aren't habits good? Absolutely. And we need habits. But behaviors are typically better. Have you ever started a new habit or routine and been really excited about it? Maybe you joined a new gym to lose weight. You went out and bought a brand new gym outfit, and a new gym bag, and a smart water bottle that tracks your water consumption. It took hours for you to put together the perfect workout playlist to go along with your brand new, fitness-focused headphones that track every calorie burned. You are ready to go. Super excited. Pumped. But that's the problem. How long will that excitement last? All of the new things become old things, which get boring. And how long will it be before you start to see any major results? It doesn't happen overnight, so will your excitement hold you long enough for the results to show up and start motivating you again? The good news is that behavior doesn't rely on that same novelty or excitement to keep you going. It comes naturally and almost unconsciously.

The loss of motivation is known as habit decay, and there are things that can accelerate decay in both habits and behaviors. One of the strongest accelerators is environmental changes, like if you change jobs, or move to a new city, or a new house. But even minor changes like extended travel or schedule changes. Any of these events can trigger habits to fall apart faster. They're just like drift multipliers, pushing you down faster. One of the best examples of this was from a 2010 study published by psychologist Philippa Lally and her research team[14]. They monitored participants as they tried to build simple daily habits like walking and drinking more

---

[14] Lally, P., Van Jaarsveld, C. H., Potts, H. W., & Wardle, J. (2010). How are habits formed: Modelling habit formation in the real world. European Journal of Social Psychology, 40(6), 998–1009.

water. But what they were more interested in observing is what happened to those habits when chaos got involved. Researchers found that when minor disruptions like illness, travel, and unexpected events, entered the participants' lives, those habits were instantly weakened. Even if they had been steady habits built up over months. Those automatic habits that felt like stone could crumble into dust with a single case of the flu, or a trip overseas. Watch out for environmental changes and be extra conscious of your habits and behaviors when they happen.

Both behaviors and habits share a similar problem we touched on earlier, but it's arguably even worse with behaviors. Speed. The negentropic behaviors you're creating are small and insignificant, which is what makes them so incredibly successful. But it's also what slows the results from appearing. That's why there's such an advantage that it doesn't have to depend on motivation to keep it going. Sure, you have to wait longer, but waiting isn't the hardest part, because you're waiting in silence. Frictionless behavior doesn't create stress, so it becomes effortless to wait. But you have to remember that you can never stop waiting! If you give up, and decide early that it "just isn't working, so why keep going?" you may end up just like the miner who sold his mine right before it struck gold. But the difference here is, this system isn't back-breaking work like mining for gold, so why would you ever stop?

Chapter 12: The Effect of Identity

Identity seems to be a more and more important topic in society. Who we are and what we identify as can unite or divide us. Or limit us. Weaken us. Permit us to allow drift to take over and thrive. A perfect example is this book you're reading. When I first had the idea for this book, I felt like I had a great concept, but there was a problem. *"I'm not a writer."* That's what I told myself. That's who I identified as. Not as someone who had never written before, but as someone who could never write anything good.

If I had just left it there, you wouldn't be reading these words right now. The task itself seemed overwhelming and I knew the chance of any financial return was zero… so it was just for me. For fun. But overwhelming tasks and fun don't really seem to go together. So if I had continued, and tried to just start writing the book from scratch, I probably would have written a few chapters over a couple months, and then drift would have slowly set in. Daily writing would become weekly writing, and strong concepts would be wasted by weak execution. But instead I decided to focus on two things. Changing my identity and making the big seem small. I wasn't someone who couldn't write, instead, I told myself I was a "first-time writer." And instead of trying to write the entire book, I started by just making the frame. The basic foundation, and breaking things into smaller bite-sized categories, then attacking those fragments in the order that felt the most comfortable. It made the seemingly impossible tangible. Now my new identity aligned with the negentropic behaviors I created to push me forward.

If your identity doesn't align with those behaviors, problems can arise. Those negentropic behaviors won't stick. Let's say I have a really busy day. I know that a "true writer" would find the time to write a page or two no matter what. But remember, I'm not a writer. So who cares if I skip a day. And since I already skipped yesterday, what's one more? Does this sound familiar? Now I've created a *new* behavior: Skipping my writing time. But that's probably ok with me because "I'm not a writer" anyway. The identity I've created gives me a pass to allow drift to take effect. Maybe for you it's not "I'm not a writer"… maybe it's "I'm not an athlete," and that's what's keeping you from going to the gym. Or maybe it's, "I'm bad with finances," so your head is stuck in the sand just like mine was.

A great example of identity shaping behavior happened back in the 1960s, in a small town in Austria. There was a skinny little kid who was obsessed with bodybuilders, and although he would work out occasionally, he never took exercise seriously. He certainly didn't *identify* as a bodybuilder himself… until one day he did. He started telling himself and the people around him that he was a bodybuilder, and that one day he would be the greatest bodybuilder in the world. He started to embody the lifestyle that he'd once envied. He made training his life's purpose and quickly climbed the local and national standings. Within a few years, that skinny Austrian kid had not only become the greatest bodybuilder in the world, he became a seven-time Mr. Olympia Champion, a major Hollywood actor, and the Governor of California. In *Arnold: The Education of a Bodybuilder*[15], Schwarzenegger describes how that turning point came when he started consciously seeing himself as a bodybuilder. Once the identity was set, everything else followed. From then on, he only did what a bodybuilder would do: he ate like a bodybuilder, trained like a bodybuilder, and kept a bodybuilder's schedule. Those negentropic behaviors became the easy path, which meant he didn't have to

---

[15] Schwarzenegger, A. & Hall, D. (1977). Arnold: The Education of a Bodybuilder. Simon & Schuster.

rely on constant motivation or willpower. He was simply living the identity he had chosen.

But what happens when success itself goes against your identity? Tragedy can unfold even if you succeed. Kurt Cobain started playing with Nirvana in the Seattle underground grunge scene in the late 1980s. His self-image was of someone who hated record labels and the mainstream rock stars he saw topping the charts on MTV. He felt they were posers, destroying the true anti-establishment soul of rock. So when Nirvana blew up and started topping the charts themselves, Kurt had an identity crisis. That inner conflict of an anti-establishment rocker going mainstream contributed to his development of severe depression. Unfortunately, he ended up taking his own life, and many people believe his tragic fate was connected to his identity conflicting with the life he was thrust into.

Identity itself isn't inherently good or bad, nor am I saying that you should abandon any identity that conflicts with your goals. You should, however, be aware of how identity is controlling your inner voice and how it can effortlessly drive you toward your goals, or drift you away from them. Reflect on what labels you have given yourself as your personal identity. Write these identities down and list the characteristics they have, or feelings that they give you. Pay attention to the positive, negative, or neutral connotation associated with those characteristics. If you start to see a pattern that your list is mostly negative, you should consider reframing how you identify with the world and yourself. Reframing can be as easy as going from, "I'm not a good writer" (negative) to "I'm a learning first-time writer" (neutral/positive). Reframing isn't lying to ourselves or others. Both of the statements I made can be true, but the way they're framed focuses on the negative or positive of the truth.

Chapter 13: Maintaining a Negentropic Life

In this book, you've seen how drift can sneak into the background and chip away at the foundation of your life. But you've also learned that negentropic behaviors can be achieved through small, easy, and consistent actions, and that those micro-behaviors push back against the constant force of drift. Analyzing your life to identify those actions will simplify the task of creating negentropic behaviors. You also now know to forgive yourself when drift inevitably works its way back into your life. You didn't fail. This is simply a force of nature reacting with human nature. It's unavoidable, and in alignment with the natural order of the universe. But you can't throw up your hands and say, "It's not my fault, so I give up." You still have a responsibility. Use the knowledge and tools you gained from this book to navigate through the drift and build a life that's stable and ordered.

Now that you have the knowledge and tools to fight drift, your first step should be to reflect. Reflect on your identity. How you see yourself and what your inner monologue is telling you. Does that identity line up with your goals? Is that identity chained to you for life, or can you abandon it if you want to? What would be an identity that would line up with your goals? And once you have found the identity that you want to be, start vocalizing it in your inner and outer speech. Acceptance is the only way that you will feel the identity and the behaviors will follow naturally.

Your next step should be to focus on a single topic: mind, body, relationships, or finances. Pick the one that seems like the biggest trouble area. Then focus your attention on finding your single dirty dish. Find the thing that starts your system to drift. Once you've found it, you can look for a small, almost insignificant, micro-behavior that will give you an incremental advantage to stop that drift from growing. And once you've implemented that behavior, move on to the next.

I know people are built differently, and what works for some won't work for others. So it's up to you to figure out what system works best to implement negentropic behaviors. But some people don't know where to start, or are just looking for a simple structured system. If that's you, here is an easy 4-week starter plan to get you going. Although each step probably doesn't require a week to complete, using the full time and reflecting on it daily will make the system more efficient.

Week 1: Make a Dish List

The first step is gaining the information to create negentropy. You do that by finding opportunities in each category. First, Mind; Recognize mental drift, clutter in your surroundings, attention-stealing distractions. Write down these moments. Next is Body; Look for areas of improvement. Is it your weight, sleep, energy levels. Write down the things that are hindering that improvement. Then, Relationships; This section will have two parts: finding previous relationships that need to be repaired, and actions that are neglecting your current relationships. Finally, Finance; Start tracking small purchases that add up to create chaos. Look for excess waste. Is there any spending that feels chaotic? Once you've made a "dish list" with every dirty dish in every category, then you can start creating negentropic behaviors to counter them.

Week 2: Map Your Plan

Go to your dish list of your first category and grab the one that jumps out at you. The one that you wish wasn't there, causing the most friction in your life. We're not going to implement any behaviors right now; we're just going to make a list of possible behaviors. This is a 'no bad idea' list where you should write anything that pops into your mind. You're looking for quantity, not quality at this point. Later you'll narrow it down to practical actionable behaviors. Do this for each category and work through each item.

Week 3: Start the Shift

The list you made last week needs to be narrowed down. Remove any behavior that isn't small enough, easy, and can be done consistently. If it feels like a lot of work, it's too big. Implement the smallest behaviors first. One at a time, not all at once. After you have a new behavior that feels natural you can then start to expand to the next one in a different category. The reason you want to do these individually and slowly is so you can be conscious of the behavior and how it's integrating with your life. Don't focus on the results. Those won't show themselves for a while. Right now you're focusing on making sure this behavior can become a part of your life without friction. This week will feel slow, but that's exactly how it should feel.

Week 4: Rinse and Repeat

This next step isn't just for week 4… it's for every week that follows too. You need to be constantly re-evaluating your drift, making new dish lists, and creating new negentropic behaviors. Every week, have a "drift check", where you gauge how much drift has entered your life in each category. You'll never have to worry about finishing the task of identifying drift and creating systems because the drift will never stop coming. Just like gravity, it's a never-ending force that has been pushing against you since birth. The difference is that now you are better equipped with tools to fight back. Time to start fighting.

Acknowledgements

A special thanks to DAVE for being there to help, any time of the day